DOWNHILL SKIING
FOR FUN!

By Jessica Deutsch

Content Adviser: Stacey Gerrish, Training Manager, Beaver Creek Ski & Snowboard School, Accredited Trainer,
Children's Examiner, and Member of the Children's Education Training Team,
Professional Ski Instructors of America—Rocky Mountains, Edwards, Colorado
Reading Adviser: Susan Kesselring, M.A., Literacy Educator, Rosemount-Apple Valley-Eagan (Minnesota) School District

Compass Point Books ✛ Minneapolis, Minnesota

Compass Point Books
151 Good Counsel Drive
P.O. Box 669
Mankato, MN 56002-0669

This book was manufactured with paper containing at least 10 percent post-consumer waste.

Photographs ©: Oshchepkov Dmitry/Shutterstock, cover (left); Blaz Kure/Shutterstock, front cover (right), back cover; Bibliotheque Nationale, Paris, France/Archives Charmet/The Bridgeman Art Library, 4; Mikael Damkier/Shutterstock, 5; Val Thoermer/Shutterstock, 6; mumbojumbo/Shutterstock, 7; Jan Bruder/Shutterstock, 8; Steve Rosset/Shutterstock, 9; Gary Blakeley/Shutterstock, 10; Olga Bogatyrenko/Shutterstock, 12 (top); 2happy/Shutterstock, 12 (middle); titelio/Shutterstock, 12 (bottom); Karon Dubke/Capstone Press, 13 (top, middle left); Greenland/Shutterstock, 13 (middle right); Achim Prill/iStockphoto, 13 (bottom left); Hulton Archive/Getty Images, 13 (bottom right); Stephen Coburn/Shutterstock, 14; PitorSikora/iStockphoto, 15; Onur Kocamaz/iStockphoto, 16; Anders Sellin/iStockphoto, 17; Photodisc, 18, 19, 21, 37, 47; Lisa Kyle Young/iStockphoto, 20; anderm/Shutterstock, 23; Brian Chase/Shutterstock, 23; Maksym Gorpenyuk/Shutterstock, 25; Walter Quirtmair/Shutterstock, 26; prism_28/Shutterstock, 27; Ilja Mašík/Shutterstock, 29; Photography by Gary Potts/Shutterstock, 30; Jani Bryson/iStockphoto, 31; Chris Zawada/iStockphoto, 32; Kris Lindahl/AP Images, 34; Gaetan Bally/Keystone/AP Images, 35; Audrey Stenkin/iStockphoto, 36; Alex Kuzovlev/Shutterstock, 38; Brian Firestone/Shutterstock, 39; Mike Powell/Allsport/Getty Images, 40; Steve Powell/Allsport/Getty Images, 41; The Granger Collection, New York, 42 (top); IOC, Olympic Museum/Allsport/Getty Images, 42 (bottom); FPG/Hulton Archive/Getty Images, 43 (left) Pascal Pavani/AFP/Getty Images, 43 (right); Denis Pepin/Shutterstock, 44; Devendra M. Singh/AFP/Getty Images, 45.

Editor: Brenda Haugen
Page Production: Heidi Thompson
Photo Researcher: Marcie Spence
Art Director: LuAnn Ascheman-Adams
Creative Director: Joe Ewest
Editorial Director: Nick Healy
Managing Editor: Catherine Neitge

Library of Congress Cataloging-in-Publication Data
Deutsch, Jessica, 1981–
  Downhill skiing for fun! / by Jessica Deutsch.
      p. cm. — (For Fun!: Sports)
  Includes index.
  ISBN 978-0-7565-4028-9 (library binding)
1. Skis and skiing—Juvenile literature. I. Title.
  GV854.315.D48 2009
  796.93′5—dc22   2008037569

Visit Compass Point Books on the Internet at www.compasspointbooks.com
or e-mail your request to custserv@compasspointbooks.com

Table of Contents

Note: In this book, there are two kinds of vocabulary words. Skiing Words to Know are words specific to downhill skiing. They are defined on page 46. Other Words to Know are helpful words that are not related only to downhill skiing. They are defined on page 47.

A Winter Tradition

It's hard to imagine that skis were once just wooden planks with leather straps. But people have been skiing for more than 4,000 years. They started long before plastic, steel, or other ski materials were invented. People used what they had to make skis. Wood and bark from trees and leather from animal hides were their best materials.

Skis were first used as transportation during the snowy months of the year. Today downhill skiing is a favorite winter sport for many people. They choose to go skiing in their free time—for vacations, weekend outings, and whenever they can get to a ski slope.

Best of all, skiing is something you can do by yourself or with others. Either way, get ready for some snowy winter fun!

Something for Everyone

Different styles of skiing call for different types of skis. When skis were first invented, they looked a lot like today's Nordic, or cross-country, skis (right). Nordic skiers cover long distances on trails. The toes of their boots are attached to the skis, but the heels remain free. Free-heel skiing allows a skier to move more easily on flat ground as well as ski uphill.

Freestyle skiing

In the 1800s, mountaineers in the Swiss Alps began to use their cross-country skis to ski downhill. Alpine—or downhill—skiing was born.

Today skiers enjoy several forms of downhill skiing. Traditional downhill skiers follow the fall line—the most direct route down a ski slope. Freestyle skiing is a combination of alpine techniques and acrobatics. Telemark skiing combines elements of Nordic and alpine skiing. Telemark skiers crisscross down hills on skis with free heels—much like the Nordic skis. Some skiers prefer to ski in the wilderness, away from resorts and crowds. This is called backcountry skiing.

Resorts and Beyond

Skiing is a great way to get fresh air and see amazing scenery during the winter months. Ski resorts are found in places that have cold, snowy climates and mountainous or hilly landscapes. If you're lucky, you might live close to one of these resorts. Some people travel great distances to ski at certain resorts because the slopes are exciting and the scenery is beautiful.

Each ski resort has several ski trails, or runs. Each trail is different. Some are long, steep, and difficult. Others may be easier, less steep, and shorter.

The snow on each trail is groomed and packed down to provide smooth and safe skiing.

Some skiers prefer off-trail skiing (below). These backcountry skiers go in small groups to remote summits. There they can enjoy the quiet of the mountainous country. Some skiers go to great lengths to reach these slopes. Heli-skiing refers to skiing in remote mountain areas reached by helicopter.

From Ski Tip to Ski Boot

Alpine skis tend to be wider and heavier than other kinds of skis. They have metal edges to help you turn at high speeds or carve through the snow. Alpine skis have an hourglass shape.

The tip is the front end of your ski. On some skis, the tip forms a point. The tail is the back end of your ski. The tail is usually the same width as the tip and is square at the end. Twin-tip skis—used by freestyle skiers—have a tip at the front and at the back. This allows freestyle skiers to ski backward.

Alpine skis vary in length and width. Experience, body weight, height, skiing style, and skiing terrain will determine the length of ski that you use. Experts at shops selling and renting ski equipment can help you choose the right skis.

A binding attaches to the boot. Most alpine bindings are easy to use. They are attached to the ski and close when the skier steps into them. They are designed to release when a skier falls.

Alpine ski boots have two parts—a hard, plastic, leak-proof outer shell and a soft, warm inner boot. Finding boots that fit well is important. Pinching and points of pressure are signs that your boots are too tight. Boots that are too loose can make it more difficult to handle your skis. Wearing wool ski socks will help with your boot fit and make your feet feel more comfortable. Ski boots are not easy to walk in, but good-fitting boots will make skiing more fun.

Renting Equipment

If you are a beginner and don't own skis, renting equipment is your best bet. However, you may want to buy your own boots to make sure they fit well and are comfortable. The fit of your boots, bindings, and skis can greatly affect how you ski. If you rent any equipment, give your skis and poles a quick test. Trade in ill-fitting equipment for comfortable gear.

Weatherproof Fashion

You've now got your boots and skis, but you'll need a few more things before you're ready to hit the slopes.

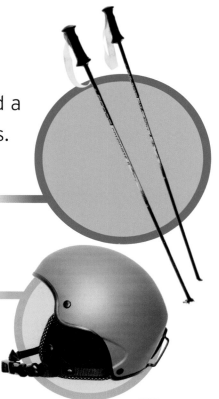

Poles: Most skiers find that poles help with turns and general balance.

Helmet: A helmet keeps your head warm and protects you when you fall.

Sunglasses or goggles: If you have sensitive eyes, you may want to wear sunglasses to protect your eyes from the sun and the bright white glare of the snow. Goggles work well, too. Goggles help keep the sun, wind, and snow out of your eyes.

Sunscreen and lip balm: Even in cold temperatures, you should use sunscreen to protect your skin from the sun. Wearing lip balm will protect your lips from the sun, cold, and wind.

Gloves or mittens: Don't forget to protect your hands. Gloves or mittens keep them warm during a long day on the slopes.

Outerwear: Skiers need to wear layers of warm clothing and waterproof outerwear to keep them comfortable and dry.

That Was Then

Most skiers choose outerwear designed for skiing. But in the late 1800s and early 1900s, the dress code was more formal. Men wore suits and button-up shirts. Women wore long dresses, jackets, and hats.

Approaching the Slope

Experienced skiers can make the sport look easy. But for a beginning skier, standing at the top of a slope can be scary.

Most ski resorts offer lessons for skiers at all levels. An instructor can show you skiing techniques, offer safety tips, show you how to use the chairlift, and guide you through ski runs.

Beginners often take skiing lessons before hitting the slopes.

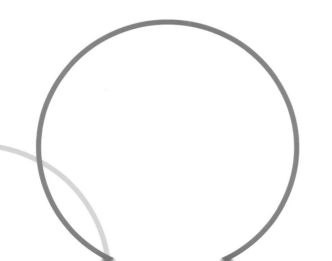

Each skier learns at his or her own pace. And each skier has different goals. You might take a couple of lessons when you first start skiing. Or you might take many lessons over a long period. Advanced skiers take lessons throughout their lives to improve their techniques.

Walking, Gliding, and Turning

Wearing skis for the first time can feel weird. Stiff boots, long skis, and layers of winter gear can make even simple movements difficult. Take time to adjust to your skis before hitting even the easiest slopes.

First, practice getting in and out of your ski bindings. Find a patch of flat ground, and place your skis down on the snow. Put your toes into the tops of the bindings. Push your heels down into the bindings until the bindings click. To get out of your skis, press

the levers or buttons on the bindings. This should release your boots from your skis.

Next, try a neutral stance wearing your boots and skis. Stand with your knees slightly bent. Spread your weight evenly between the right and left sides.

Before you do any skiing, you should be comfortable gliding and walking in your skis. Slide your skis back and forth. Lift your right ski, then the left. Hop from one foot to the other. To walk, place your left arm forward as you step with your right ski and your right arm forward as you step with your left ski.

Take a Turn

Try a "star" turn. Lift your right ski (below). Turn it slightly to the right before stepping down. Bring your left ski parallel to the right one. Be careful not to tangle the backs of your skis as you turn. Repeat until you have turned one complete circle.

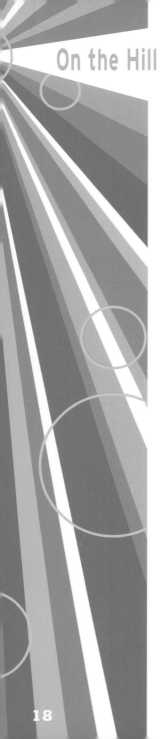

Use Your Edge

Skiing is based on elements that help a skier turn on the hill. By now you have noticed that stiff bindings keep your heels attached to your skis. A secured heel can make basic movements tough, but it makes control much easier.

Another element is the metal edges of your skis. In all turns, you'll use your edges. Find the edges on your skis. The inside edge is beneath the inside of your foot. The outside edge is beneath the outside of your foot.

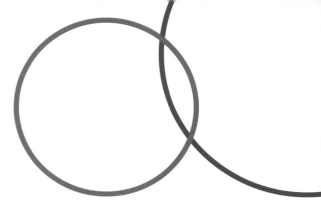

Practice shifting your weight to the edges of your skis. In a turn, the inside ski will be on its outside edge, and the outside ski will be on its inside edge.

When you are able to move more freely, make your way to the beginners' area, or bunny hill.

Snowplow

With practice, skiers are able to move down a hill with speed, control, and balance. Stopping and turning are important moves for a skier. Beginning skiers use several techniques to do this. The most basic is the snowplow, or wedge turn.

To slow down, bring the tips of your skis close together and the tails apart. As you do this, you will bring more weight to the inside edges of your skis. To stop, push the tails of your skis farther apart and keep your ski tips pointed together (above). Your skis will create a natural brake.

Let's do a quick check-in with your body before you begin. Create a wedge shape with your skis. Balance

your weight equally over both skis. Flex your ankles. You will feel your shins against the fronts of your boots. This will help keep your weight over the balls of your feet, which makes turning easier.

To make a right turn, steer your left ski to the right. As you extend your left leg, be sure to keep your skis in the wedge position.

Pressure or tension will build on your left (outside) ski. Come to a gentle stop using your wedge braking technique.

Test your control using your snowplow. Go down a gentle slope, and switch between slowing down, turning left and right, and braking.

Taking a Tumble

Wipeout. Biff. Face plant. Skiers have many ways to say "fall." This is because falling is a part of skiing.

A fall can happen for many reasons. You might lose your balance. Your skis might become tangled. You might fall to the side to avoid another skier in your path. All skiers fall on the hill. It's how well you can avoid injury and hurting others that matters.

The key to falling safely is staying relaxed. If your body tenses as you hit the ground, you are more likely to get hurt. Avoid putting your hands down to catch your

Getting Up After a Fall
Lie on your belly on the snow. Place your skis out to either side of you, forming a V shape. The ski tails should make the point of the V. Push yourself up with your hands and arms.

fall—this might lead to a sprained wrist or a broken bone. After you fall, you will have to find your skis, poles, and any lost articles of clothing. Place your skis across the hill, not pointing downhill. Put on the ski that is farthest down hill, and then put on the other one.

Parallel Turns

Snowplow skiing teaches you all the basic movements—but with limited speed. As you become more experienced, parallel turns—turning with the ski tips and tails the same distance apart—will help you move more smoothly and quickly down the hill.

Parallel turns build on what you already know. When you were just a snowplow skier, you mainly used your outside ski for steering. The move to parallel skiing requires that you use your inside ski, too. As you move down the hill, practice using both your inside and outside skis to steer your turns. Begin down the hill in the snowplow position. Extend your outside ski tail. You will feel pressure build on this ski. Transfer the pressure from your outside ski to your inside ski by turning your inside thigh outward. This motion should draw your skis parallel.

Next, try to project your hips forward as you move into a turn. This will give you a little lift and take some weight off the skis. It will also allow you to move onto the inside edges of your skis and turn. Also, try steering your skis with your lower body. As you move down the hill, your shoulders should face downhill more than your skis do.

Stringing together these techniques requires a mix of balance, control, and steering. Be patient—and practice, practice, practice!

Lifts, Tows, and Cable Cars

Most resorts have one or more mechanical lifts to help skiers reach the top of each hill. Resorts often post signs with instructions for each lift, but here is an idea of what to expect.

With a tow rope and T-bar, you never lose contact with the ground. A rope will pull you up a hill. A T-bar (right) will push you up a hill. Either way, you will wear your skis and keep your ski tips pointing forward.

Another way to get up the hill is by chairlift (above)—a seat attached to a moving cable that carries you up the hill. A person will help you get on the chairlift by holding the chair as you sit down. Keep your ski tips forward and still as you ride. Be sure to stand up as you get out of the chairlift.

And be careful. Chairlift exiting areas can have a lot of traffic.

Cable cars and gondolas are the easiest of all the lifts. Remove your skis and carry them. Stand—or sit—and enjoy the view!

Snow

One of the biggest challenges in skiing is learning how to deal with various snow conditions. The possibilities are endless! Snow changes with the wind, temperature, sun, altitude, and season. Like all natural factors, snow is both awesome and unpredictable.

Snow called powder is often found in the high altitudes of mountains. Powder is light and dry. It makes skiing easy because you can turn your skis with little effort.

Corn snow refers to snow that has melted and refrozen into small clusters. Corn snow is common in the spring. Skiers like it because it creates fast and easy skiing conditions. But you'll have to get out early in the day to enjoy corn snow. It can turn slushy under the warmth of the sun.

When heavy snow is bumpy and hard-packed, it's
called crud or junk snow. This type of snow is less ideal
for skiing because it's uneven and can quickly turn to
ice. Icy ski conditions are difficult—even dangerous.
Skiers can expect to do a lot of skidding on icy snow.

Be Prepared

Before you head out to ski, make sure you are ready for the day's weather. Cold temperatures and wind chills can make for dangerous skiing situations. If your skin is exposed to extreme cold for too long, you might begin to notice frostbite—grayish patches of flesh. If you start to feel numb, sleepy, or dizzy and find speaking difficult, you might have hypothermia. This

serious condition occurs when your body loses more heat than it produces. To help prevent frostbite and hypothermia:

- Dress right for the temperature and wind chill.

- Take regular breaks for water, snacks, rest, and warmth. Hot chocolate and tea are perfect ways to warm up before heading to the slopes again.

In some areas, avalanches are another safety hazard on the slopes. An avalanche is a large mass of snow and ice that suddenly moves. Many resorts do avalanche testing and set up signs to keep skiers away from dangerous areas.

Know Your Surroundings

A ski slope can be a popular, crowded place. To make skiing enjoyable for everyone, follow the rules posted by the ski resort. Here are rules skiers should always follow.

- Maintain control over your speed. Only choose ski runs that you can manage.

- Observe all signs on the slopes.

- Never ski off the marked trails, even if you see other skiers doing so.

- Yield to slower skiers and skiers in front of you.

- When taking a new trail, look around to be sure it's safe and clear.

- When you need to stop on a ski run, stop on the side, not in the middle. Avoid stopping just over the crest of a hill where it might be hard for approaching skiers to see you.

Reading the Signs

Slopes are usually marked with signs to tell skiers the difficulty and steepness of each run. It's important to stick to the runs that you can complete safely.

 Easy trails are marked with a green circle.

 A blue square marks more difficult, intermediate trails.

 A black diamond marks the most difficult trails for nonexperts.

 A double diamond marks trails for expert skiers.

 A triangle with an exclamation point means that you should proceed with caution.

Teamwork

Joining a ski club or a ski team is a good way to enjoy skiing and learn more about the sport. You will have a chance to hear your teammates' skiing tips and share your own.

Another benefit is training with a coach. He or she will offer advice on how to improve your technique and help you build confidence in your skiing abilities.

Ski clubs often participate in local ski competitions. Some even have advanced skiers who travel to various cities to compete.

Want to Race?

There are many types of alpine races. Some of these races focus on speed. Others focus on control.

Skier passing a gate

Speed is the name of the game in downhill and the super giant slalom events. In both races, the skier tries to make it from the top to the bottom of the course with the fastest time. In downhill, racers keep a tucked position as they ski the long course. These racers can reach speeds up to 60 to 90 miles (97 to 145 kilometers) per hour. In super giant slalom, there are about 30 gates on a course that is slightly shorter than the downhill course. The skier does less gliding and more turning on the super giant slalom course.

Control is the name of the game in slalom and giant slalom. These are considered technical events because a racer must make tight turns to stay within the gates. Unlike downhill and super giant slalom, the slalom events have many gates that are very narrow. If skiers miss a gate, they are disqualified. Slalom is a shorter race with 40 to 75 speed gates spaced tightly together. Giant slalom has a longer course than the slalom and more space between gates. The number of gates for giant slalom varies from course to course.

The true test of an alpine skier is the combined event. The times from a slalom and downhill course are added together for a final time.

Twists, Turns, and Tricks

Are you a show-off by nature? If so, freestyle skiing might be for you. But beware! Freestyle is for the bravest of skiers.

Some freestyle skiers enjoy taking on moguls—a series of mounds or bumps of snow that are placed closely together down a ski slope. In advanced mogul competitions, racers also complete jumps. Racers are scored by a group of judges who look at style, speed, and technique.

Moguls

In the aerial event, a skier speeds down a kicker, or ramp, and is launched about 50 feet (15 meters) into the air. The skier does twists and somersaults before landing on the ground. Aerial competitors are scored on takeoff, form, and landing by a group of judges. This is a dangerous event. Aerial competitors often practice on a trampoline or in a pool before trying their tricks on skis.

Freestyle skiing seems to be adding new events all the time. The halfpipe is a U-shaped slope where skiers perform daring tricks and are judged for their style. In skier-cross, several skiers barrel down a course at the same time. With many sharp turns and obstacles on a crowded slope, skiers do all they can to stay upright—and finish first. Big air competitions are a lot like aerials— but bigger, faster, and more dangerous.

Halfpipe

Among the Best

Few athletes have enjoyed as much glory as Alberto Tomba, an Italian skier who specialized in slalom. Tomba earned many medals in international competitions. He won five medals at three Olympic Games. He also earned 50 World Cup victories. His explosive skiing style won him the nickname La Bomba, which is Italian for "the bomb."

And the Winner Is ... Alberto "La Bomba" Tomba

Alberto Tomba

1988 Calgary Olympics: gold medals in slalom and giant slalom

1992 Albertville Olympics: gold medal in giant slalom and silver medal in slalom

1994 Lillehammer Olympics: silver medal in slalom

1996 World Championships: gold medals in slalom and giant slalom

50 World Cup victories from 1986 to 1998

Picabo Street grew up in Triumph, Idaho, a town of just 35 people. Triumph is near the Sun Valley ski resort. Street started skiing at the age of 6. Her parents and coaches quickly realized that she was a talented skier.

A mouthy and stubborn person, Street wasn't an easy athlete to coach. In 1990, she was asked to leave the U.S. Ski Team's summer training camp because she lost her sense of commitment. But a determined Street trained until the team would take her back—and she came back full force. After winning some junior competitions, she made a big breakthrough. At the 1993 World Championships, she won a silver medal in the combined event. Among many other honors, she won a silver medal in downhill at the 1994 Olympics and a gold medal at the 1998 Olympics in super giant slalom.

Name Game
Picabo means "shining waters" in the language of the Shoshone and Bannock Indian tribes.

Picabo Street

What Happened When?

2500 B.C.   **1850**   **1860**   **1870**   **1920**   **1930**

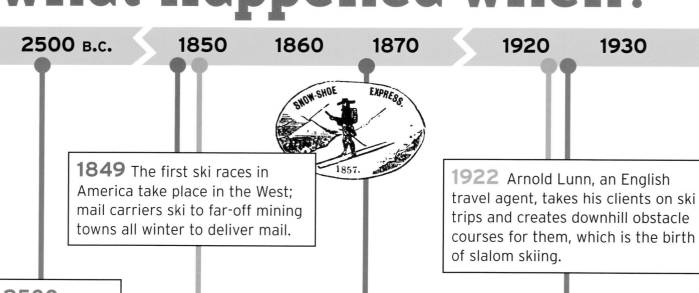

1849 The first ski races in America take place in the West; mail carriers ski to far-off mining towns all winter to deliver mail.

1922 Arnold Lunn, an English travel agent, takes his clients on ski trips and creates downhill obstacle courses for them, which is the birth of slalom skiing.

2500 B.C. People from Norway to Mongolia use wood and leather skis as transportation.

1868 Sondre Norheim of Norway uses stiff bindings that hold down his heel to win a skiing race.

1924 Chamonix, France, hosts the first Winter Olympics with four skiing events.

1850 The first Nordic ski race is held in Oslo, Norway.

1940   **1950**   **1960**   **1970**   **1980**   **1990**   **2000**   **2010**

1948 In St. Moritz, Switzerland, Gretchen Fraser is the first American to win a gold medal in an Olympic alpine skiing event.

1971 The first national freestyle competition takes place in Waterville Valley, New Hampshire.

1988 The super giant slalom makes its debut as an Olympic event.

1992 The first freestyle event, moguls, is added to Olympic competition in Albertville, France.

1952 The Olympic Committee adds giant slalom as an event.

2006 American Julia Mancuso wins a gold medal in the giant slalom at the Olympics in Turin, Italy.

2008 Americans Lindsay Vonn and Bode Miller capture the overall World Cup titles.

43

Fun Skiing Facts

In 1909, Carl Howelsen brought ski jumping to the Barnum & Bailey Circus. Millions of people visiting the circus saw Howelsen speed down a greased ramp and jump 40 feet (12 m) into the air.

In 1936, Sun Valley resort in Idaho opened with the first chairlift. The chairlift was designed by Jim Curran, a railroad engineer for Union Pacific. He based his invention on the aerial cables he built for transporting bananas in South America.

More than 58 million visits to ski resorts are recorded each year.

In 1970, Japanese skier Yuichiro Miura attempted to ski nearly 8,000 vertical feet (2,438 m) down Mount Everest, the world's tallest mountain. Miura successfully skied 6,600 feet (2,012 m)—then fell. He slid about 1,300 feet (396 m) after his fall. In 2003, Miura starred in a documentary called *The Man Who Skied Down Everest*.

Jackson Hole, located in the Teton mountain range in Wyoming, is the tallest alpine ski area in the United States. It has a vertical drop of 4,139 feet (1,262 m).

Climate change and global warming affect skiers and the ski industry. In 2000, the National Ski Area Association realized resorts were feeling the effects of less snow. It started a program called Sustainable Slopes. As part of the program, several ski resorts have pledged to invest in environmentally friendly business practices to "keep winters cool."

Skiing Words to Know

aerial: freestyle event that involves skiing off a ramp and performing acrobatics

alpine: style of skiing that involves skiing downhill

backcountry: off-trail skiing

big air: extreme, freestyle aerial skiing event

binding: ski part that keeps the boot heel and toe attached to the ski

bunny hill: beginner area at a ski resort

chairlift: moving cable with benches or seats that carries skiers up a mountain

combined: event that tests a skier's slalom and downhill ski-racing ability

crud: uneven snow surface combined with ungroomed snow

fall line: most direct route down a ski slope

free-heel skiing: cross-country and alpine skiing in which the heel is not attached to the ski

freestyle: type of alpine skiing that involves tricks and artistry

gates: poles that show racers the course they must follow

halfpipe: U-shaped snow trench used by skiers for tricks

heli-skiing: type of backcountry skiing in which helicopters drop off skiers in remote mountainous areas.

kicker: ramp for an aerial event

mogul: freestyle event that consists of a series of small bumps or mounds

parallel turn: type of turn in which both skis are side by side

powder: light, fluffy snow

resorts: ski areas with groomed trails, lifts, and services

slalom: race in which a skier must go through gates

snowplow: basic method for controlling speed and direction

star turn: standing turn that makes a star shape in the snow as the skier turns in a circle

tail: back end of a ski

T-bar: lift that is made of a moving cable and a T-shaped bar

telemark: style of skiing that combines techniques from alpine and cross-country skiing

tip: front end of a ski

tow rope: lift that is made of a moving cable and a handle

Other Words to Know

disqualified: eliminated from competition for breaking a rule

frostbite: skin damage caused by exposure to cold

hypothermia: serious condition in which a person's body temperature begins to drop

summit: top or peak of a mountain

terrain: ground or landscape

wind chill: measurement of the combined effect of temperature and wind speed

Where to Learn More

More Books to Read

Dippold, Joel. *Picabo Street: Downhill Dynamo*. Minneapolis: Lerner Publications, 1998.

Mason, Paul. *Skiing*. Chicago: Heinemann Library, 2003.

Smith, Warren. *Go Ski*. New York: DK Publishing, 2007.

On the Road

U.S. National Ski and Snowboard Hall of Fame and Museum
610 Palms Ave.
Ishpeming, MI 49849
906/485-6323

Colorado Ski Museum
231 S. Frontage Road
Vail, CO 81567
970/476-1876

On the Web

For more information on this topic, use FactHound.
1. Go to *www.facthound.com*
2. Choose your grade level.
3. Begin your search.
This book's ID number is 9780756540289
FactHound will find the best sites for you.

INDEX

ABOUT THE AUTHOR

Jessica Deutsch first stepped into a pair of skis when she was 9 years old. She continues to enjoy downhill skiing as well as other winter sports. An avid reader, Deutsch lives in Minneapolis, Minnesota, and works in publishing.